# GATEWAY TO THE PACIFIC

# Vancouver

## JILL FORAN

**Published by Weigl Educational Publishers Limited**
6325 – 10 Street SE
Calgary, Alberta, Canada
T2H 2Z9
Web site: http://www.weigl.com

**National Library of Canada Cataloguing in Publication Data**
Foran, Jill.
 Vancouver

 (Canadian Cities)
 Includes Index
 ISBN 1-894705-65-3

 1. Vancouver (B.C.)--Juvenile literature. I. Title. II. Series:
Canadian Cities (Calgary, Alta)
FC3847.33.F67 2001          j971.1'33          C2001-911388-9
F1089.5.V22F67 2001

Printed and bound in the United States of America
1 2 3 4 5 6 7 8 9 0   05 04 03 02 01

**Senior Editor**
Jared Keen
**Copy Editor**
Heather Kissock
**Design**
Warren Clark
**Cover Design**
Terry Paulhus
**Layout**
Bryan Pezzi
**Photo Researcher**
Tina Schwartzenberger

We acknowledge the
financial support of
the Government of
Canada through the
Book Publishing
Industry Development
Program (BPIDP) for
our publishing activities.

**Photograph Credits**
Every reasonable effort has been made to trace ownership and to obtain permission to reprint copyright material.
The publishers would be pleased to have any errors or omissions brought to their attention so that they may be
corrected in subsequent printings.

Cover: Al Harvey; Inside Cover: Al Harvey; BC Archives: page 7B (PDP00810); City of Vancouver Archives: pages
6M (CVA 677-182), 7T (DVA 677-734), 8T (LGN 457), 9M (LGN 463); Harper Collins: page 11R; Guys and Dolls/The
Vancouver Playhouse Theatre Company/Photo by David Cooper: page 12T; Corel: page 27B; Andrew Dawson: page
10L; Mark Gilbert/Vancouver International Film Festival: page 13B; Denise Grant: page 11L; Al Harvey: pages 3TL,
3ML, 3B, 4, 5M, 5B, 9B, 10R, 12M, 13T, 14, 15, 16, 17, 18T, 18B, 19T, 19B, 20T, 20B, 21L, 22T, 22B, 23B, 24, 25,
26T, 27T, 28T, 28B, 29L, 30; Courtesy of the BC Lions: page 21R; National Archives of Canada: page 8B (PA-
044978); Photofest: page 29R; Tourism Vancouver: pages 23T, 26B; Vancouver Police: page 8M; Washington State
Historical Society: page 6B.

# Contents

# Introduction

Vancouver is the largest city in British Columbia. It is located in the southwestern part of the province, where it sits on a **peninsula.** The peaks of the Coast Mountains serve as Vancouver's backdrop, while sandy beaches and lush forests line the city's borders.

Vancouver

Canada

0    500 km

## Getting There

There are many ways to get to Vancouver. Several airlines fly to the Vancouver International Airport each day. BC Rail and VIA Rail provide train service to the city, while BC Ferries and various cruise ships bring visitors in via the waterways. You can drive to Vancouver on the Trans-Canada Highway or on a number of other roads.

# At a Glance

## Climate

Vancouver has one of the mildest climates in Canada. The Coast Mountains shield the city from the cold north wind, and warm breezes blow in from the Pacific Ocean. Both the mountains and the ocean contribute to the city's pleasant climate. Snow rarely falls in Vancouver, and the temperature almost never drops below freezing. The average daily temperature in January is 2° Celsius. Winters in Vancouver are so mild that flowers are often blooming by February. In the summer, the city enjoys warm, sunny days. The average daily temperature in July is 17°C.

Vancouver is known for its many rainy days, which are common throughout all the seasons. Rain helps keep the city fresh and green.

## Area & Population

The City of Vancouver occupies 114 square kilometres on the south shore of Burrard Inlet. About 545,000 people live in the city, and about 1.5 million more live in the surrounding areas. The Vancouver metropolitan area is made up of the city itself and the many communities that encircle it. Known as Greater Vancouver or the Lower Mainland, this metropolitan region includes Burnaby, Port Coquitlam, Coquitlam, New Westminster, North Vancouver, and various other municipalities.

## Gateway to the Pacific

Vancouver is situated on a beautiful natural harbour. The Burrard Inlet harbour is connected to the Pacific Ocean via English Bay, the Strait of Georgia, and Juan de Fuca Strait. The waters that surround the city never freeze, making it possible for ships to sail into the harbour at any time of the year. Vancouver's proximity to the Pacific Ocean has made it one of the busiest ports in North America, and by far the busiest port in Canada. The city has earned the nickname "Gateway to the Pacific."

## Interesting Statistics

**1.** Greater Vancouver is the third-largest metropolitan area in Canada.

**2.** Almost half of British Columbia's entire population lives on the Lower Mainland.

**3.** Vancouver is situated 42 km from the U.S. border.

**4.** Vancouver is linked to four major railways.

**5.** Vancouver was the site of the 1986 World's Fair. Called Expo 86, the fair attracted more than 22 million tourists from around the world.

# The Past

## Early Settlement

Native Peoples were the first to inhabit the area that is now Vancouver. Long before European explorers arrived in the region, the Coast Salish were living in villages on the shores of Burrard Inlet and the Fraser River.

In 1792, a British naval officer named Captain George Vancouver arrived in Burrard Inlet. He charted the area and then claimed it for Britain. Still, it was well into the nineteenth century before Europeans began to settle there.

The area's first permanent European settlement was established in the 1860s when a logging village grew up around Hastings Mill. In 1867, an English sailor named John Deighton opened a **saloon** near the sawmill. Deighton was nicknamed "Gassy Jack" because he was so talkative. His saloon was popular with the settlers, and soon the entire community became known as Gastown. In 1869, Gastown was officially incorporated as the town of Granville.

In 1884, the Canadian Pacific Railway (CPR) decided that the town of Granville would be the site of its western **terminus**. The general manager of the CPR suggested that the town be named after George Vancouver to attract investors and settlers from Britain. In 1886, the town of Granville became the City of Vancouver. At that time, there were about 2,000 people living in the area.

*The busy harbour in Vancouver ensured steady growth for the young city in the 1800s.*

## Key Events

**George Vancouver**

**1791** Spanish explorer Jose Maria Navaez sails into Burrard Inlet.

**1792** Captain George Vancouver charts Burrard Inlet and claims the Vancouver region for Britain.

**1827** The Hudson's Bay Company establishes Fort Langley, a fur-trading post, on the Fraser River.

## The Government

The City of Vancouver held its first municipal election on May 3, 1886. Alexander MacLean, a Scottish real-estate dealer, was voted in as Vancouver's first mayor. MacLean and ten elected aldermen were responsible for governing the city. They held their first City Council meeting on May 10, 1886. On June 13 of that year, a terrible fire destroyed most of the city. Fewer than half a dozen buildings remained. Within hours of the "Great Fire," the mayor and council had developed a plan to rebuild the city. Because the fire had destroyed most of Vancouver's buildings, City Council had to meet in a tent for several months. By the end of 1886, Vancouver had about 800 new buildings, including a new City Hall on Powell Street.

*Alexander MacLean helped lay the foundation for Vancouver's municipal government.*

In 1888, David Oppenheimer became the second mayor of Vancouver. He is considered to be one of the city's greatest mayors. During the three years that he held office, he brought streetcars to the city, initiated street paving, officially opened Stanley Park, and founded a number of schools. He also developed a lighting company and the city's first civic water supply.

Vancouver's municipal government is still responsible for much of the city's lighting and for its water supply. It is also responsible for housing, sewage, garbage, recycling, and air-quality control. Today, Vancouver's City Council consists of a mayor and ten councillors.

**1867** Jack Deighton opens a saloon near Hastings Mill on Burrard Inlet. The entire community becomes known as Gastown.

**1869** Gastown is incorporated as the town of Granville.

**1884** The CPR announces its plan to make Granville the western terminus of its transcontinental railway.

## Law and Order

Vancouver's first police officer was appointed on May 10, 1886. Chief John Stewart was also granted an assistant, who acted as jailer. The jailer's job was to look after the prisoners, who were kept in a cell that had been added on to the constable's cottage.

The Vancouver Police Force grew to include three more officers in June of 1886. After the Great Fire destroyed most of the city, Mayor Alexander MacLean appointed Jackson T. Abray, V. W. Haywood, and John McLaren as constables. The mayor hoped that these men would help clean up the city and

*Early law enforcers had few resources with which to fight crime.*

maintain order in the aftermath of the fire. Chief Stewart now had a police force to lead. At first, the officers had no uniforms, but each was given a temporary badge made from a silver dollar.

The constables' cottage was destroyed in the fire, and as a result, the police force worked out of the same tent that served as City Hall. There was no jail in the tent, so prisoners were chained to a tree stump that stood nearby.

The Vancouver Police Department has grown substantially since 1886. Today, the department has hundreds of officers and a number of police stations throughout the city.

*Vancouver's police department patrols not only the city streets but also the waterways.*

## Key Events

**1886** The town of Granville becomes the City of Vancouver. A city council and the Vancouver Police Department are formed.
    The Great Fire rips through the city, destroying most of the buildings and killing several people.

**1887** The first CPR train reaches Vancouver.

**1891** Canadian Pacific Steamships sail between Vancouver and Asia for the first time.

# Early Transportation

The CPR was responsible for developing much of Vancouver. In order to gain railway and shipping access, the CPR cleared and paved many of the city's streets, and built impressive railway yards. The first CPR train chugged into Vancouver from eastern Canada in 1887. Over the next few years, the city began to **boom** as more trains brought many people and products to the area.

*By the beginning of the twentieth century, Vancouver had more commercial and financial importance than Victoria.*

In 1891, the steamships of the Canadian Pacific fleet began to sail between Vancouver and Asia. The **efficiency** of these ships helped to establish Vancouver as a major world port. Along with the steam trains, the ships contributed to the rapid growth of the city's population and industry.

## The Depression and World War II

Like the rest of Canada, Vancouver suffered severely during the Great Depression of the 1930s. The city's unemployment rate was high. It continued to grow as thousands of people from other parts of Canada travelled to Vancouver in search of work and a milder climate. Unrest among the unemployed caused many riots and protests in the city. Angry demonstrators demanded that the provincial and federal governments do something about working conditions. It was the outbreak of World War II that brought an end to the high unemployment rates and suffering economy. Jobs in war-related industries were created almost instantly. People in the city found work in shipbuilding, the manufacturing of aircraft parts, and construction.

**1908** The University of British Columbia is founded.

**1930s** Vancouver suffers through the Great Depression and becomes the site of many protests against working conditions and unemployment.

**1986** Vancouver hosts Expo 86 and celebrates its 100th birthday.

# Famous People

## Joy Kogawa
## 1935—

Joy Kogawa is a celebrated novelist and poet. She was born in Vancouver to Japanese parents. After Japan bombed Pearl Harbor in 1941, British Columbians of Japanese descent were treated as potential enemies. As World War II raged and fear of an enemy attack increased, thousands of Japanese Canadians were sent to **internment** camps. Joy and her family were among these people. They were sent to a camp in Slocan, British Columbia, and then to Coaldale, Alberta.

This difficult experience left a lasting impression on Joy. Her novel *Obasan* focuses on the injustices suffered by Japanese Canadians during World War II. *Obasan* was very well received, and it has won several literary awards. It has also helped bring attention to the problems and tragedies of discrimination. Joy has written two other novels, *Istuka* and *The Rain Ascends*. She has also published many celebrated poems, essays, and children's books.

## David Suzuki
## 1935—

David Suzuki is one of Canada's most influential scientists. Born in Vancouver, David and his family went on many camping trips. These early experiences helped to form David's love of nature.

After graduating from high school, David earned

*David Suzuki is Canada's best-known environmentalist.*

a degree in biology and a Ph.D. in zoology. In 1963, he became a zoology professor at the University of British Columbia. He soon gained international recognition for his research in **genetics**. Later, David began to focus on nature and conservation. Because of his work, David has been awarded twelve honorary degrees, the UN environmental medal, and a Governor General's Award for conservation.

*Joy Kogawa was awarded the Order of Canada, the nation's highest honor.*

# Kim Campbell
# 1947–

Kim Campbell is perhaps best known as Canada's first female prime minister. Kim was born in Port Alberni, BC, but her family moved to Vancouver when Kim was very young. In 1988, she became a member of the federal Conservative party, and by 1990, she was Canada's first female justice minister. In 1993, she became the first woman Minister of National Defence. That same year, Prime Minister Brian Mulroney announced his retirement, and Kim was encouraged to run for leader of the Conservative party. She won the election that June, becoming not only the first woman to lead the federal Conservative party, but the first woman to lead the country as well. Kim served as Canada's prime minister from June 1993 to November 1993.

*After serving as prime minister, Kim went on to teach politics at Harvard University.*

*In addition to his writing triumphs, Douglas has won several design awards.*

# Douglas Coupland
# 1961–

Douglas Coupland is a well-known writer and artist. He was born on a Canadian military base in Germany, but his family moved to Vancouver when he was 4 years old.

A magazine article he wrote in 1988 led to his first novel, *Generation X: Tales for an Accelerated Culture*. The book was an instant success, and it brought Douglas international recognition as a writer. He has gone on to write eight more books, including *Shampoo Planet*, *Microserfs*, and *Polaroids From the Dead*.

# Bryan Adams 1959–

Bryan Adams is one of Canada's most celebrated rock and roll stars. Bryan's family moved from Kingston, Ontario, to Vancouver when he was fourteen. By the age of eighteen, he was signed to a recording contract. In 1984, his fourth album, *Reckless*, brought him a large international following. By the end of the 1980s, Bryan had won many awards, including several Junos. Since the 1980s, Bryan has released other successful albums, including *Waking Up the Neighbours* (1991) and *18 Til I Die* (1997). Throughout his career, Bryan has sold more than 50 million albums worldwide. He still has a home in Vancouver.

# Culture

## The Arts

Vancouver's arts scene is both exciting and wide-ranging. The city has thirty-two professional theatre groups and many impressive theatrical venues. Among Vancouver's many theatres are the Arts Club Centre, the Playhouse, and the Firehall Arts Centre. These theatres present a variety of plays, from Canadian dramas and comedies to well-known Broadway musicals.

For music lovers, the Vancouver Symphony Orchestra performs at the Orpheum Theatre, and the Vancouver Opera Association performs at the Queen Elizabeth Theatre. Annual music festivals, such as the Du Maurier International Jazz Festival and the Vancouver Folk Music Festival, always draw large crowds.

People who appreciate visual arts can visit one of the city's many art galleries. The most celebrated is the Vancouver Art Gallery. Housed in the city's old courthouse, the Vancouver Art Gallery showcases artwork by Canadian and international artists. One popular exhibit features the work of Emily Carr, a well-known Canadian painter. Many of Emily Carr's paintings were inspired by the natural beauty of British Columbia and by the strong cultural presence of the province's coastal Native Peoples.

*Vancouver has a thriving theatre scene. Hundreds of plays are performed in the city each year.*

### FESTIVALS

Vancouver hosts a variety of festivals each year. Among the many celebrations is the **International Children's Festival**, which takes place in May. This popular event is held in Vanier Park and features live theatre, concerts, dance presentations, storytellers, and puppet shows.

**The Bard on the Beach Festival** runs from June until late September. This festival presents a selection of Shakespeare's plays

# Celebrating the Holidays

Throughout the year, citizens and visitors take part in various holiday celebrations. On July 1, people gather for one of the largest Canada Day celebrations in the country. The Canada Place Pier hosts an all-day party that begins with the swearing-in of new citizens and continues with music and dance acts performed throughout the day. At the end of the celebration, fireworks light up the Vancouver sky.

In December, Vancouver glows again—this time with thousands of Christmas lights. One of the most popular displays is the Festival of

*The first Vancouver Polar Bear Swim took place in 1920. Since then, the event has grown from 10 participants to more than 2,100.*

Lights at VanDusen Garden. More than 19,000 lights decorate a section of the garden, and people throughout the city come to see the festive display.

On New Year's Eve, thousands of Vancouverites attend the First Night Festival. This festival rings in the new year with an assortment of outdoor performances and activities. Hundreds of people celebrate New Year's Day by taking part in the annual Polar Bear Swim. This chilly event consists of a quick swim in the icy waters of English Bay. The swim is believed to bring good luck for the year ahead.

performed in open-ended tents. It, too, is held at Vanier Park.

**The Pacific National Exhibition** begins in late August. It is the largest agricultural fair in British Columbia, and it features everything from rodeos and livestock shows to a large midway and carnival games.

**The Vancouver International Film Festival** takes place in September and October, and presents more than 300 films from about 50 countries. It is considered one of the largest film festivals in North America, and it runs for fourteen days.

19TH VANCOUVER INTERNATIONAL FILM FESTIVAL

SEPT 22 TO OCT 5 2000

LANET. DIFFERENT WORLDS.  AIR CANADA  AGF  VISA

*On New Year's Eve, thousands of Vancouverites attend the First Night Festival.*

# All Kinds of Food

People in Vancouver enjoy many types of food. Fresh fruits and vegetables are harvested from nearby orchards and farms, and the city's surrounding waters provide an abundance of fish and seafood. Vancouver's many ethnic communities also provide a wide range of interesting treats. The Punjabi Market has many restaurants that serve traditional samosas or curry dishes. The market also has spice shops and candy stores that sell delicious Indian treats. In Chinatown, diners can taste a variety of unique foods, including chicken feet and shark-fin soup.

*Vancouver's Punjabi Market offers a dazzling array of food from India, Pakistan, Bangladesh, Sri Lanka, Uganda, and East Africa.*

Vancouverites enjoy eating out. There are more than 3,000 restaurants in the city, providing a near-endless variety of dining options. Italian, French, Greek, Mexican, Indian, Chinese, and Japanese eateries are all found in the city. In fact, Vancouver is considered to be one of the most **cosmopolitan** restaurant cities in North America. Many of Vancouver's restaurants also serve vegetarian meals and West Coast dishes, such as fresh salmon.

## Lemon-Dill Salmon

1 whole salmon, cleaned
45 mL (3 tbsp) olive oil
1 bunch fresh dill
1 large lemon, sliced
salt and pepper

Rub the salmon with olive oil, inside and out. Sprinkle with salt and pepper. Place lemon slices and dill sprigs inside the salmon. Wrap the salmon in aluminum foil, and bake at 200°C for 40-45 minutes.

*There are more than 3,000 restaurants in the city, providing a near-endless variety of dining options.*

# Cultural Groups in Vancouver

Vancouver is one of the most **ethnically diverse** cities in Canada. People from North America, South America, Asia, Africa, Europe, and Australia contribute to Vancouver's rich cultural scene.

More than 200,000 people of Chinese descent live in the city. The first Chinese immigrants arrived in the Vancouver area for the Fraser Valley Gold Rush in 1858. Then, during the 1880s, more Chinese people arrived to help build the Canadian Pacific Railway. Descendants of the early immigrants continue to live in Vancouver, while other Chinese people have immigrated more recently. Much of the Chinese population lives or works in Chinatown. Vancouver's Chinatown is the largest in Canada and the second largest in North America, after San Francisco's. Many lively celebrations, including Chinese New Year, are held in Chinatown every year.

Other ethnic groups in Vancouver include people of European descent, such as Germans, Scandinavians, Ukrainians, French, and Italians. About one percent of the city's population is of Native descent.

*Chinese New Year is a two-week-long celebration. Parades and performances can be seen throughout Chinatown.*

## The Museum of Anthropology

The Museum of Anthropology is located on the University of British Columbia campus. It houses more than 30,000 cultural objects and 200,000 archaeological **artifacts** from around the world. More than half of the museum's entire collection has come from the First Nations of coastal British Columbia. Native artifacts on display include gold and silver jewellery, sculptures, bone carvings, canoes, and ceremonial masks. The museum also houses one of the world's largest collections of totem poles and woodcarvings. The Museum of Anthropology has helped to create an appreciation for the achievements of the province's First Nations and of other cultural communities throughout the world.

# The Economy

## A Port City

Vancouver is the chief financial, industrial, and shipping centre of Canada's West Coast. It is also the economic heart of British Columbia. Most of the province's industry is based on mining, fishing, and forestry. Vancouver processes and ships the materials that are produced from these activities. There are approximately 2,000 factories in Greater Vancouver, including mills, fish-processing plants, and oil refineries. These factories produce about $2 billion worth of goods every year and employ more than 70,000 people. Almost all of the province's major industrial companies have their headquarters in Vancouver.

Many of the goods manufactured in Vancouver are exported via the city's port. Vancouver has long been known as the Canadian gateway for all cargo coming from and going to Asia. More than $9 billion of goods from BC alone are shipped to Asia each year. The port of Vancouver also ships goods to

> *Vancouver's port is one of the most efficient in North America.*

non-Asian countries, including the United States, Brazil, Australia, and New Zealand. It imports a variety of goods as well. More than 3,000 ships from about 90 countries visit the port of Vancouver each year. The port is one of North America's busiest, handling about 70 million tonnes of cargo annually. Its many terminals are connected to a vast network of railways, highways, airways, and shipping lanes, making the port one of the most efficient in North America.

*Every day, huge ships deliver tonnes of goods to and from Vancouver.*

# Tourists and Filmmakers

Tourism is one of Vancouver's fastest growing industries. Every year, more than 8 million visitors from around the world travel to Greater Vancouver. Many people head to the city to take in its many tourist attractions, while others travel there on business. Vancouver is one of Canada's leading convention hubs. Hundreds of business conventions are held there each year. The city has an assortment of hotels, restaurants, stores, and attractions to meet the needs of all its visitors. There are also eleven cruise-ship companies that use Vancouver as their home port. These companies offer cruises to Alaska and attract nearly 1 million passengers each year. Tourist spending in Vancouver generates about $3 billion annually, and the tourism industry employs more than 70,000 people.

Tourists are not the only ones attracted to Vancouver's beautiful location. Filmmakers are also drawn to the city's scenery. Vancouver is one of North America's leading film-production centres, and many movies and television shows have been shot in the area. The city's film industry generates more than $2 billion dollars annually and employs about 25,000 people. Canada's largest film and television studio facility, Lion's Gate, is in North Vancouver. Several film and video companies and talent agencies are also located within the city.

*A cruise-tour gives visitors a unique view of Vancouver.*

# Getting Around Vancouver

There are a number of ways to get around in Vancouver. The city has an excellent public transportation system called Translink. Electric trolley buses and regular buses follow a variety of routes throughout Greater Vancouver. A rapid transit system, called the SkyTrain, runs for 29 km and connects downtown Vancouver with Burnaby, New Westminster, and Surrey. These aboveground SkyTrains have no drivers. Instead, they are monitored by computers at SkyTrain headquarters. The last of Vancouver's public transit services is the SeaBus. The SeaBus consists of two 400-passenger **catamaran** ferries that cross Burrard Inlet and connect the downtown core to North Vancouver. The ferries take only twelve minutes to travel from one point to the other.

For those who prefer cycling or walking, Vancouver has several designated bicycle lanes and pathways. The city's downtown area is very compact, making it easy to get around

*SkyTrains whisk citizens and visitors to a number of sites around the Vancouver area.*

on foot. Many Vancouverites walk, cycle, or take public transit to avoid the city's frequent traffic jams.

> **SkyTrains have no drivers. Instead, they are monitored by computers.**

## BC Ferries

BC Ferries is one of the largest ferry systems in the world. It is made up of forty vessels and serves forty-six destinations. Some of these ferries transport passengers from Vancouver to destinations such as Vancouver Island, the Gulf Islands, and the Sunshine Coast. The ferry trip between Vancouver and Vancouver Island is one of the most popular. The scenery throughout this trip is beautiful. Tree-covered shorelines and lonely islands are seen along the way, and whales are often spotted in the well-travelled waters.

# Education

Vancouver is a major centre for education. The city has about 100 public elementary schools, 20 public high schools, and 40 private or church-supported schools. The public school system also supports the Vancouver School of the Arts and the Vancouver Vocational Institute. The Vancouver School Board's education programs are constantly growing to meet the needs of the city's thriving population. A wide range of programs are now offered, including French and Mandarin immersion, English as a second language, and courses for the hearing and visually impaired.

Vancouver also has a variety of post-secondary institutions. The University of British Columbia is Vancouver's oldest university. It is also one of the largest in Canada, with more than 34,000 students. Simon Fraser University has a campus in Burnaby, and one in downtown Vancouver. More

*The University of British Columbia was founded in 1908 and opened in 1915.*

than 25,000 students are enrolled in classes at Simon Fraser. The city's newest university is the Technical University of British Columbia. It opened in 1999 to provide students with training in advanced technology. The BC Institute of Technology has earned an international reputation for the quality of its programs. Vancouver is also home to the Emily Carr Institute of Art and Design, one of the country's most celebrated art schools.

*Simon Fraser University offers over 100 programs for students to study.*

# Sports and Recreation

## Recreation

Vancouver's location and mild climate make it a great spot for outdoor recreation all year round. The city's park system provides its residents with a variety of facilities, including tennis courts, swimming pools, golf courses, lawn bowling greens, and hiking trails. Vancouver also has many ocean walkways and scenic bicycle paths. Sandy beaches can be found along English Bay, and swimming is a common activity during the summer. Vancouver's many waterways also provide opportunities for kayaking, sailing, windsurfing, white-water rafting, and scuba diving.

*Sailboats dot the beaches and waterways around Vancouver.*

Skiing and snowboarding are popular activities during the winter months. Three ski hills are just a short drive from the city's downtown. Grouse Mountain and Mount Seymour Provincial Park are located in North Vancouver. Both hills provide more than twenty challenging downhill runs, as well as a number of cross-country skiing and snowshoeing trails. Skiers and snowboarders can also tackle the slopes and trails at Cypress Bowl Provincial Park, which is located in West Vancouver.

*Grouse Mountain has been a welcome winter getaway since 1926.*

## Professional Sports Teams

Vancouver is home to a number of professional sports teams. The BC Lions have been part of the Canadian Football League since it was formed in 1956. They play their home games at BC Place Stadium, where thousands of fans cheer them on. The Vancouver Canucks have been a team in the National Hockey League since 1970. They are based at Vancouver's General Motors Place.

The Vancouver Whitecaps are part of the American Professional Soccer League. They play their home games at Swangard Stadium.

*Professional sporting events are popular in Vancouver, regardless of the season.*

## The BC Sports Hall of Fame and Museum

Canada's largest sports museum is in Vancouver's BC Place Stadium. The BC Sports Hall of Fame and Museum honours the province's many athletes, and it features a number of galleries that celebrate sports in British Columbia. The History Gallery takes visitors on a trip through time, tracing the history of sport from 1890 to the present. Photos, trophies, and old equipment are all found in this gallery. There are also videos that replay some of the province's greatest moments in sports. The Discovery Gallery shows visitors what it takes to be a professional athlete, and the Hall of Champions tells the stories of BC's athletic triumphs. In the Participation Gallery, visitors can test their own athletic skills in a number of hands-on activities. They can climb a rock wall, arm wrestle with the arm-wrestling machine, race along a 14-metre track, or throw a baseball to see how fast it travels. The museum also has galleries dedicated to First Nations sport, coaches, and referees, and two of the province's most inspiring athletes: Terry Fox and Rick Hansen.

# Tourism

## Stanley Park

One of Vancouver's most popular attractions is Stanley Park. Situated only minutes from the downtown core, Stanley Park is the third largest urban park in North America. It encompasses 405 hectares of flowering gardens, dense forests, and several lookouts that offer spectacular views of the city, the mountains, and the ocean. Visitors to the park will find an endless range of things to see and do. The park is home to many attractions, including the Children's Farmyard and Miniature Railway, a pitch-and-putt golf course, a water park, tennis courts, an ocean-side swimming pool, totem poles, and an outdoor theatre. There are also three beaches in Stanley Park, as well as many prime areas for viewing wildlife. An 8.5 km seawall surrounds a portion

*Stanley Park was named in honour of Lord Stanley of Preston, a former governor general of Canada.*

of the park and provides visitors and residents with a scenic pathway for walking, running, cycling, and inline skating.

The Vancouver Aquarium is also located in Stanley Park. It is the largest aquarium in Canada, housing more than 8,000 marine animals, such as dolphins, whales, sea lions, and otters. The aquarium offers a number of educational programs and tours. Visitors can learn about marine life, study habitats, and even stay overnight!

*The seawall around Stanley Park took nearly sixty years to build.*

*The Capilano Suspension Bridge attracts more than 800,000 visitors each year.*

# Capilano Suspension Bridge

Vancouver's oldest tourist attraction is the Capilano Suspension Bridge. The first bridge to span the rushing Capilano River was constructed in 1889 by a wealthy man named George MacKay. He built the bridge in order to gain access to the rest of his 2,400 hectares of property. Made of cedar planks and hemp rope, the bridge was known as the "Laughing Bridge," and it became a popular tourist destination. The Laughing Bridge has since been replaced with the present Capilano Suspension Bridge. It is still made of cedar, but steel cables have replaced the hemp rope.

The Capilano Suspension Bridge is considered to be the world's longest pedestrian bridge, stretching 135 m in length and hanging about 70 m above the river. As tourists walk along the swaying overpass, they can watch kayakers battling the white water below. After crossing the bridge, visitors can explore hiking trails, walk among towering evergreens, and see traditional totem poles.

## The Lookout

Tourists who want to get a spectacular view of Vancouver can visit The Lookout at Harbour Centre Tower. At 174 m high, the Harbour Centre Tower is the tallest building in British Columbia. Two glass elevators on the outside of the tower bring visitors to an observation deck, which provides a bird's-eye view of the city and its surrounding areas. There is also a shopping mall at the base of the tower and a revolving restaurant at the top.

# Vanier Park

Tourists who visit Vanier Park can take in several sites in one stop. Vanier Park is located on English Bay, just west of the Burrard Street Bridge. It encompasses natural green spaces and scenic shoreline walkways. It is also home to three popular attractions: the Vancouver Museum, the H. R. MacMillan Space Centre, and the Vancouver Maritime Museum. The Vancouver Museum has a number of exhibits that display the heritage, culture, and natural history of the Lower Mainland. Historic photographs, archaeological artifacts, Native crafts, and antique toys are among the many items on display.

The H. R. MacMillan Space Centre features state-of-the-art exhibits and demonstrations. Visitors can fly through space on the Virtual Voyages flight **simulator**, or learn about the solar system in the Cosmic Courtyard interactive exhibition gallery. The Star Theatre presents laser-light and astronomy shows, and the GroundStation Canada Demonstration Theatre reveals the mysteries of space.

At the Vancouver Maritime Museum, visitors will learn about the maritime heritage of coastal British Columbia. Among the museum's exhibits are model ships, naval uniforms, and original maps from George Vancouver's ship. A restored 1928 Royal Canadian Mounted Police (RCMP) boat, called the *St. Roch*, sits next to the museum. Visitors can tour the *St. Roch*, which is now a National Historic Site.

The Maritime Museum also houses the Children's Maritime Discovery Centre. This centre features a remote-controlled deep-sea robot as well as high-powered telescopes for viewing Vancouver's present-day port life. It also houses Pirate's Cove, a pirate display that includes a ship, buried treasure, and a gallery that features some of history's most notorious pirates.

*Vanier Park provides a relaxing break from the bustle of Vancouver.*

*From the comfort of an outdoor patio, visitors to Granville Island watch ships sail in and out of the harbour.*

# Gastown and Granville Island

Two of Vancouver's most popular districts are Gastown and Granville Island. Gastown is just a short walk from the downtown core. It has some of the city's oldest buildings, many of which date back to the late nineteenth century. Visitors to Gastown can stroll along cobblestone streets and visit the many cafés, antique shops, art galleries, and souvenir stores that are part of the district. They can also see the world's first steam clock. This clock is powered by an underground steam system used to heat many of Gastown's buildings. Every 15 minutes, the clock's whistle blows, and every hour, a waft of steam rushes out.

Granville Island is located near False Creek. It is a major recreational and commercial centre, boasting a variety of shops and restaurants, several theatres, and a public market. Shoppers at Granville Island can buy everything from organic produce and baked goods to colourful hand-made clothing and artwork. Among the many recreational attractions are live theatrical performances, a water park, and an adventure playground. During special events at Granville Island, clowns, face painters, and musicians can be seen strolling throughout the district.

## Science World

Science World is located in the giant silver dome that stands at the end of False Creek. Hands-on exhibits and demonstrations at Science World help to explain some of the mysteries of science. Visitors can crawl through a beaver lodge, get up close to an active beehive, search for gold, play a tune on a giant walk-on keyboard, blow square bubbles, and create their own cyclone—all in the name of science!

# Architecture

## Arthur Erickson's Vancouver

A local architect named Arthur Erickson has designed many of Vancouver's most fascinating buildings. In many ways, he has helped to shape the look of the city. In the 1960s, Erickson began to design buildings that reflected Vancouver's climate, geography, and progressive culture. Some of his best-known structures include Simon Fraser University and the Museum of Anthropology. Located atop Burnaby Mountain, Simon Fraser University looks like a huge spaceship. Erickson, along with Geoffrey Massey, designed the main buildings of the university in 1963. These bare concrete buildings are laid out around a large courtyard. The design caused great controversy because of its strange use of space and its unusual appearance.

The Museum of Anthropology is also unusual in appearance. The design was

*Simon Fraser University is an architectural wonder.*

inspired by the **longhouses** of British Columbia's coastal Native Peoples. Large concrete beams and columns imitate the shapes of the longhouses. The enormous glass-enclosed Great Hall provides a panoramic view of the mountains and the sea, and it serves as a grand home for the towering totem poles and other artifacts that stand within. Erickson's design for the museum won a great deal of praise and several architectural awards.

*The Museum of Anthropology was designed to reflect the area's Native history and culture.*

# Vancouver Library Square

One of Vancouver's newest buildings is The Vancouver Library Square. Moshe Safdie, an accomplished Canadian architect, designed the building, and construction was completed in 1995. The library resembles the Colosseum in Rome, Italy. Although it may look a bit like an ancient structure, Library Square has many ultra-modern features. The square occupies an entire city block and includes the 9-level library, a 21-floor office building, a daycare, retail shops, and several cafés. Inside the library are thirty-five columns on each floor, 51 km of cable, and **conveyors** to take the more than 1 million library items from one section of the building to another.

*Impressive pillars support the curved walls of The Vancouver Library Square's outer concourse.*

# Canada Place

Canada Place is one of Vancouver's most recognizable landmarks. It was built to mark the city's **centennial** celebration and to house the Canadian Pavilion at Expo 86. That year, it was acknowledged as one of the best-ever host **pavilions** at a world's fair. Canada Place juts into the harbour and sits at the bottom of Howe Street. The building was designed to represent the spirit of Canada's maritime heritage and British Columbia's reputation as Canada's Gateway to the Pacific. The peaked fabric roof gives the impression

of a giant sailboat ready to set out across the waves. Today, Canada Place houses several facilities, including the World Trade Centre, a cruise ship terminal, a hotel, restaurants, retail shops, and the CN IMAX Theatre.

# Fascinating Facts

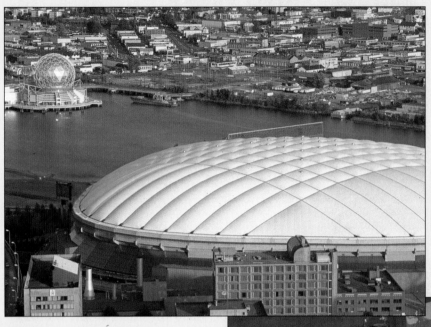

**4** The dome-shaped roof of BC Place Stadium is air-supported. It is inflated by huge fans and kept in place by crisscrossed steel cables.

**5** More than 40,000 people live in Vancouver's West End, making it one of the most densely populated neighbourhoods in Canada.

**1** The Sam Kee Building, in Vancouver's Chinatown, is considered to be the world's thinnest office building. It is only 1.5 m wide.

**2** The *St. Roch*, which is on display at the Vancouver Maritime Museum, was the first vessel in the world to make a round trip through the Arctic's fabled Northwest Passage.

**3** Because of its location, Vancouver is one of the few places in North America where you can ski and golf in the same day.

**6** In the late 1800s, Vancouver's Chinatown was known as Saltwater City.

**7** The Dr. Sun Yat-Sen Classical Chinese Garden is the only full-scale classical Chinese garden found outside of China. This beautiful terrace was designed and constructed by a team of fifty-two workers from Suzhou, China, with some help from Vancouver architects. All of the materials for the garden were shipped from China, and no modern equipment was used in its construction.

**8** More than 50 percent of Vancouver's elementary school students speak a language other than English. The main languages spoken in Vancouver, after English, are Chinese, Punjabi, Vietnamese, and Tagalog, a language spoken in the Philippines.

**9** Jason Priestley, Michael J. Fox, and Joshua Jackson are among the many well-known actors who have lived in Vancouver.

**10** Vancouver sits on top of the most active earthquake zone in Canada. Every year, there are about 300 minor tremors in the southwest region of British Columbia. In recent years, the city has spent more than $300 million on reinforcing many of its bridges, tunnels, and buildings, in case a major earthquake should occur.

*Joshua Jackson*

# Activities

Based on what you have read, choose the best answer to the following questions:

## Multiple Choice:

**1** Alexander MacLean was Vancouver's first
a. police officer
b. mayor
c. European settler
d. fireman

**2** What tragic disaster destroyed most of Vancouver in 1886?
a. The Great Fire
b. The Great Flood
c. The Great Earthquake
d. The Great Cyclone

**3** Vancouver's newest post-secondary institution is
a. The University of British Columbia
b. Simon Fraser University
c. The Technical University of British Columbia
d. The Emily Carr Institute of Art and Design

**4** Which Vancouver-based sports team plays at BC Place Stadium?
a. The Canucks
b. The Lions
c. The Whitecaps
d. The Canadians

**5** What historic Vancouver district is home to the world's first steam-powered clock?
a. Granville Island
b. Chinatown
c. Gastown
d. Stanley Park

## True or False:

**6** Vancouver is home to the second largest Chinatown in North America.

**7** The Vancouver Museum is Vancouver's oldest tourist attraction.

**8** Vancouver's SkyTrains operate without drivers.

**9** Each year on Valentine's Day, hundreds of brave Vancouverites participate in the Polar Bear Swim.

**10** The Vancouver Aquarium is one of the many museums found in Vanier Park.

Answers:
1. b
2. a
3. c
4. b
5. c
6. True.
7. False. The Capilano Suspension Bridge is the oldest attraction.
8. True.
9. False. The Polar Bear Swim takes place on New Year's Day.
10. False. The Vancouver Aquarium is located in Stanley Park.

# More Information

## Books

Foran, Jill. **Eye on Canada: British Columbia.** Calgary: Weigl Educational Publishers, 2002.

Francis, Daniel. **Copying People: Photographing Columbia First Nations 1860–1940.** Saskatoon: Fifth House Publishers, 1996.

## Web sites

**City of Vancouver**

http://www.city.vancouver.bc.ca

**Vancouver Tourism**

http://www.tourism-vancouver.org
http://www.discovervancouver.com

**Vancouver Aquarium**

http://www.vanaqua.org

Some Web sites stay current longer than others. To find information on Vancouver, use your Internet search engine to look up topics such as "Stanley Park," "Gastown," "SkyTrain," or any other topic you want to research.

# Glossary

**artifacts:** cultural objects

**boom:** experience a period of growth

**catamaran:** a boat with a frame that consists of two parallel floats

**centennial:** a 100-year anniversary

**conveyors:** moving belts that transport objects from one area to another

**cosmopolitan:** worldly

**efficiency:** being productive without wasting time or energy

**ethnically diverse:** from a wide range of cultures

**genetics:** the study of inherited characteristics

**internment:** being confined

**longhouses:** communal houses constructed by Native Peoples, consisting of a wooden framework

**pavilions:** large tents or structures that house an exhibition

**peninsula:** land that is surrounded by water on three sides

**saloon:** a bar or tavern

**simulator:** a machine that imitates

**terminus:** either end of a railway line

# Index